P9-CFE-110

Watch me grow

Bear

LONDON, NEW YORK, MUNICH,
MELBOURNE and DELHI

Written and edited by Lisa Magloff
Designed by Sonia Whillock,
Mary Sandberg and Pilar Morales

Publishing Manager Sue Leonard
Managing Art Editor Clare Shedden
Jacket Design Simon Oon
Picture Researcher Marie Osborn
Production Shivani Pandey
DTP Designer Almudena Díaz

First American Edition, 2003

Published in the United States by
DK Publishing Inc.
375 Hudson Street
New York, NY 10014

A Cataloging-in-Publication record for this book is available
from the Library of Congress.

ISBN 0-7566-0194-0

Color reproduction by
Media Development and Printing, Ltd., Great Britain
Printed and bound by
South China Printing Co, Ltd., China

Discover more at

www.dk.com

Contents

Come follow us and see how we GROW!

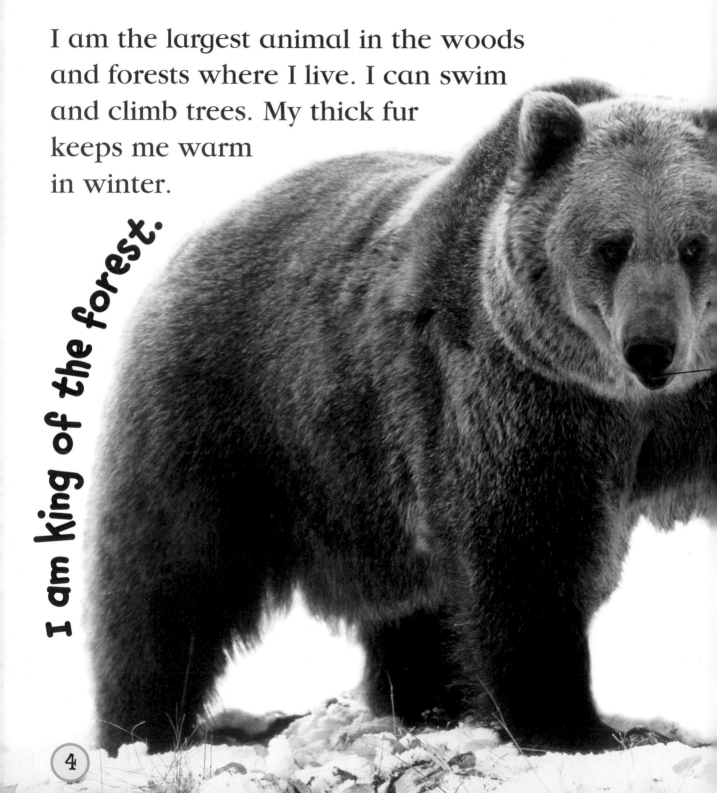

I'm a bear

I am the largest animal in the woods and forests where I live. I can swim and climb trees. My thick fur keeps me warm in winter.

I am king of the forest.

Peering around

Bears are curious. They often stand up on their back legs to look over the bushes.

Bears have long, sharp teeth and strong jaws.

The bear's sharp claws help it to hunt for food.

Turn the page and watch me grow!

Dad fights for Mom

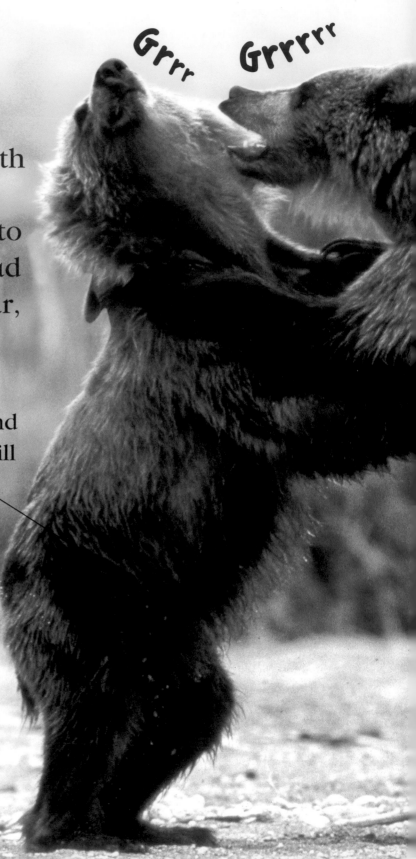

Grrr Grrrrr

Dad had to fight with other male bears to see who would get to mate with Mom. Dad was the biggest bear, so he won.

The younger and smaller bear will lose the fight.

Their fight may look scary, but these bears are not trying to hurt each other. They are wrestling to see who is the strongest.

Go away! I am the strongest.

When the cubs are born Mom and Dad only stay together for one or two weeks. Then Dad will leave and Mom will raise the cubs on her own.

Gripping facts
. . . .

🐻 Mom and Dad mate in June or July, but their cubs won't be born until the next January.

🐻 Each bear has its own area, called a territory.

🐻 Female bears can start having cubs when they are about four or five years old.

I'm born in the den

It's winter when we are born, but Mom has found a warm, snug place to protect us from the cold and snow. The place where we live is called our den.

Bald and blind
This week-old cub was born tiny, blind, and almost completely bald. It depends on its mother for everything.

During the cold winter, the mother bear does not eat. She spends all her time feeding her cubs, keeping them warm, and sleeping.

After one month, our eyes are open and we have fur.

I'm taking my first steps

After two months in the den, the weather is warmer and it's time for us to start exploring the world. We are ready to start learning all about how to be bears.

Watch and learn
Bear cubs are curious. They learn by watching Mom and by playing.

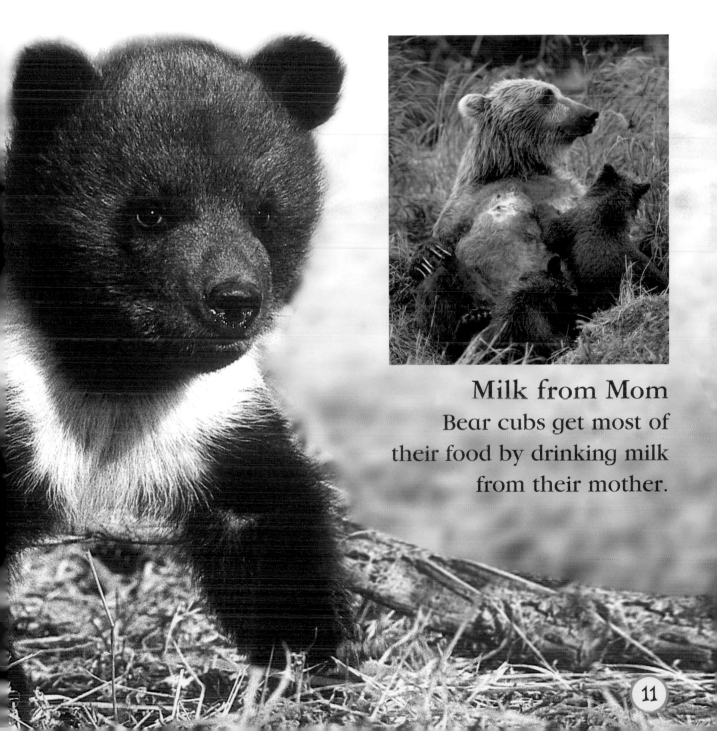

My white collar makes it easy for Mom to find me.

Milk from Mom
Bear cubs get most of their food by drinking milk from their mother.

A walk in the woods

We are three months old and very good at walking. It's time for Mom to teach us about the different foods we can find in the woods. We stay close to Mom so she can protect us.

Berry nice

The young cubs feed on berries, insects, and small animals such as frogs...yummy!

Wait for me, I'm right behind you!

The cubs have many new smells to learn about.

Bear-faced facts

🐻 Bears have a great sense of smell. They can smell food over one mile (2 km) away.

🐻 The cubs drink milk from Mom until they are about five months old.

🐻 By watching Mom carefully, the cubs learn what foods are safe to eat.

Mom is on the lookout for male bears who might hurt her cubs.

Mom on the lookout

Mom keeps watch for danger while we practice climbing trees. It's not as easy as it looks.

When she stands up, Mom can see a long way away.

Up we go...

14

...Whoops

Hold on tight!

Danger alert
A mother bear will chase off almost any danger. But hungry wolves are on the lookout for cubs that get separated from their mothers.

Wolves

I'm learning to fish

It's time for me to join the older bears for my first fishing lesson. I learn how to catch the slippery fish by watching and copying the other bears.

This six-month-old cub is too small to stand in the fast-moving water, so he fishes from the shallow water at the edge.

The bears must wait patiently for the salmon to leap out of the water.

Clams for lunch

Bears love seafood of all kinds. This mother and cub are digging for clams. Their long claws are perfect clam openers.

Time for a long sleep

Winter is here, and there is not much food to eat. It's time to find a cozy place to go to sleep. We will sleep until spring, when there is more to eat.

These are my footprints.

The bears have grown fat during summer and fall. The extra weight will nourish them until spring.

Bears grow a thick coat of winter fur.

These bears have dug a snow cave to spend the winter in.

I'm tired...time for bed.

The cubs will share their mother's den until they are almost two.

The circle of life goes round and round.

Now you know how I turned into a grown-up bear.

Here are my friends from around the world.

The Sloth Bear lives in forests in India and Nepal. Its favorite food is termites.

I'm the world's biggest bear,

The Giant Panda lives in China and eats only bamboo leaves and shoots.

These American Black Bears live in forests and don't like open spaces.

My bear friends come in all kinds of different shapes and sizes.

Spectacled Bears are from South America. They build their nests in trees.

The smallest bear is the Asian Sun Bear.

and I live in the cold, snowy Arctic.

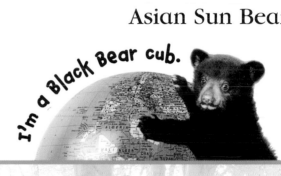

I'm a Black Bear cub.

Polar Bears' favorite foods are seals and walruses.

Friendly facts

🐻 Polar Bears are very good swimmers. They can swim for long distances without a rest.

🐻 A female bear is called a sow. A male bear is called a boar.

🐻 Bears see in color and have much better hearing and smell than humans.

Glossary

Collar
The ring of white fur around the neck of all young cubs.

Nursing
When the mother bear feeds the cubs with her milk.

Sleeping
Bears usually sleep all winter. This is called hibernation.

Salmon
A type of fish that is very fatty. It is good food for bears.

Cub
For the first year of its life, a baby bear is called a cub.

Omnivore
An animal that eats almost anything. Bears are omnivores.

Acknowledgments
The publisher would like to thank the following for their kind permission to reproduce their images:
Position key: c=centre; b=bottom; l=left; r=right; t=top.
1: Lynn Rogers; 2-3: Nature Picture Library/Tom Mangelsen; 4: Still Pictures/Klein/Hubert; 5: Corbis/Greg Probst (r), /Michael T. Sedam (cl), /Steve Kaufman (bl); Oxford Scientific Films/Mathias Breiter (tl); Lynn Rogers (br); 6-7: ImageState/Pictor; 7: Michael S. Quinton (tr); 8: FLPA - Images of Nature/L. LeeRue (cl); 8-9: Lloyd Beebe; 10: Ardea London Ltd (cl main); 10: McDonald Wildlife Photography (cl, youngest cub); 10-11: McDonald Wildlife Photography; 11: Corbis/Kennan Ward (cr); 12: Nature Picture Library/Tom Mangelsen (l); 12-13: Nature Picture Library/ Steffan Widstrand; 14: Nature Picture Library/Steffan Widstrand (c); 14-15: McDonald Wildlife Photography (c), Getty Images/J.P. Fruchet (main); 15: McDonald Wildlife Photography (c, cr);

16: ImageState/Pictor (r), McDonald Wildlife Photography (bl); 17: ImageState/Pictor (tr, l), Lynn Rogers (cr); 18: Ardea London Ltd/Stefan Meyers (c), Corbis/Dan Guravich (tl), FLPA - Images of Nature/M. Newman (tr), Still Pictures/Francois Gilson (main); 19: Ardea London Ltd/Johan De Meester (b); 20: Corbis/Joe McDonald (cr below), Team Husar Wildlife Photography (tr), ImageState/Pictor (bc), FLPA - Images of Nature/ L. LeeRue (tc), McDonald Wildlife Photography (cr above), Lynn Rogers(tl, cl, bl, br), Andrew Rouse (c); 21: Corbis/Gunter Marx Photography (foreground); 22: Lynn Rogers (tl); 22-23: Oxford Scientific Films/Daniel Cox; 23: Oxford Scientific Films/Terry Heathcote (br); Lynn Rogers (cr); 24: Nature Picture Library/Tom Mangelsen (br), Lloyd Beebe (tr), ImageState/Pictor (cl), FLPA - Images of Nature/M. Hoshino/Minden (bl), McDonald Wildlife Photography (tl).
All other images copyright DK Images